W9-AHW-217

OCT

1997

THE WORLD'S TOP TEN

DESERTS

Neil Morris

ILLUSTRATED BY VANESSA CARD

RSVP
RAINTREE
STECK-VAUGHN
PUBLISHERS
The Steck-Vaughn Company

Austin, Texas

Words in **bold** are explained in the glossary
on pages 30–31.

Text copyright © Neil Morris 1997
Illustrations copyright © Vanessa Card 1997
© Copyright 1997 Steck-Vaughn Company this edition

Published by Raintree Steck-Vaughn Publishers, an imprint
of Steck-Vaughn Company.

Editors: Claire Edwards, Helene Resky
Designer: Dawn Apperley
Picture researcher: Juliet Duff
Consultant: Elizabeth M. Lewis
Picture acknowledgements: J. Allen Cash Ltd: 15.
FLPA: 12 Eric & David Hosking, 21, 26 D. Hall, 29 top
C. Carvalho. Hutchison Library: 5 bottom, 13,
18 Christina Dodwell, 19 Dave Brinicombe, 28 top.
Images of Africa: 29 bottom. Images of India: 27. NHPA:
11 ANT, 16 Nigel J. Dennis, 22 Peter Johnson, 24 Anthony
Bannister, 28 bottom David Middleton. Still Pictures: 5 top
Cyril Ruoso, 8 Frans Lemmens, 9 Bios/George Lopez,
14 Stephen Pern, 17 Bios/Martin Gilles, 23 Foto
Natura/Martin Harvey. Tony Stone Images: 10 Ken
Stepnell. Telegraph Colour Library: 20. Trip: 25 T. Noorits.

Library of Congress Cataloging-in-Publication Data
   Morris, Neil.
   Deserts / Neil Morris : : illustrated by Vanessa Card.
      p.   cm. — (The world's top ten)
   Includes index.
   Summary: Presents information about the location,
features, and human and animal inhabitants of the ten
largest deserts in the world, including the Sahara, the
Taklamakan, the Sonoran, and the Thar.
   ISBN 0-8172-4341-0
   1. Deserts — Juvenile literature. [1. Deserts.] I. Card,
Vanessa, ill. II. Title. III. Series.
GB612.M675   1997
910'.02154 — dc20   96-11726
                                                     CIP AC

Printed in Hong Kong
Bound in the United States
1 2 3 4 5 6 7 8 9 0   00 99 98 97 96

Contents

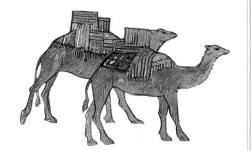

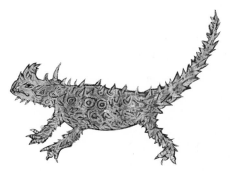

What Is a Desert?

A desert is an area of land where very little rain falls. This means that the ground is dry nearly all the time. Most deserts are in warm parts of the world. We often think of them as being covered with endless **sand dunes**. But there are many other desert **landscapes**, including rocky hills and flat, stony **plains**. Most scientists agree that any region that has less than 10 inches (25 cm) of rain a year can be called a desert.

Mountains

Rocky upland

Plain

Dry valley

Rock pillars

Stony plain

Oasis

Sand dunes

Scrub

Hot deserts

Most of the world's largest deserts are very hot places. The largest desert of all, the Sahara in Africa, has temperatures that reach 122°F (50°C). In hot deserts the temperature usually falls very fast at night, sometimes by as much as 45°F (25°C).

In spite of their heat, temperature changes, and lack of water, deserts are not empty **wastelands**. Many kinds of plants and animals live in this difficult **environment**. Some people live in deserts, too.

This dry, rocky area is a common desert landscape in the Negev region of southern Israel.

The biggest deserts

In this book we take a look at the ten biggest deserts in the world. We see where they are, how different they are from each other, and learn something about the people and animals who have made the desert their home.

Cold wilderness

Not all deserts are as hot as the Sahara. The Gobi, in Mongolia, is also very cold in the winter. The Arctic and Antarctica can also be called deserts. These areas are so cold that there is little rainfall. Any water instantly freezes. The icy wastes around the North and South poles get bigger in the winter and smaller in the summer.

Baking heat in the summer and freezing cold in the winter have helped shape the stony hills of the Gobi, the world's fourth largest desert.

5

The Biggest Deserts

This map shows the ten biggest deserts in the world. Although we show them clearly on the map, the edges of a desert are not as clear as the borders of a country or the coastline of an island. Many of the world's deserts are growing very slowly. This process is called **desertification**.

The World's Top Ten Deserts

1	Sahara	3,250,000 sq mi
2	Australian	600,000 sq mi
3	Arabian	500,000 sq mi
4	Gobi	400,000 sq mi
5	Kalahari	200,000 sq mi
6	Taklamakan	125,000 sq mi
7	Sonoran	120,000 sq mi
8	Namib	116,000 sq mi
9	Kara Kum	105,000 sq mi
10	Thar	100,000 sq mi

NORTH AMERICA

Sonoran Desert

ATLANTIC OCEAN

SOUTH AMERICA

PACIFIC OCEAN

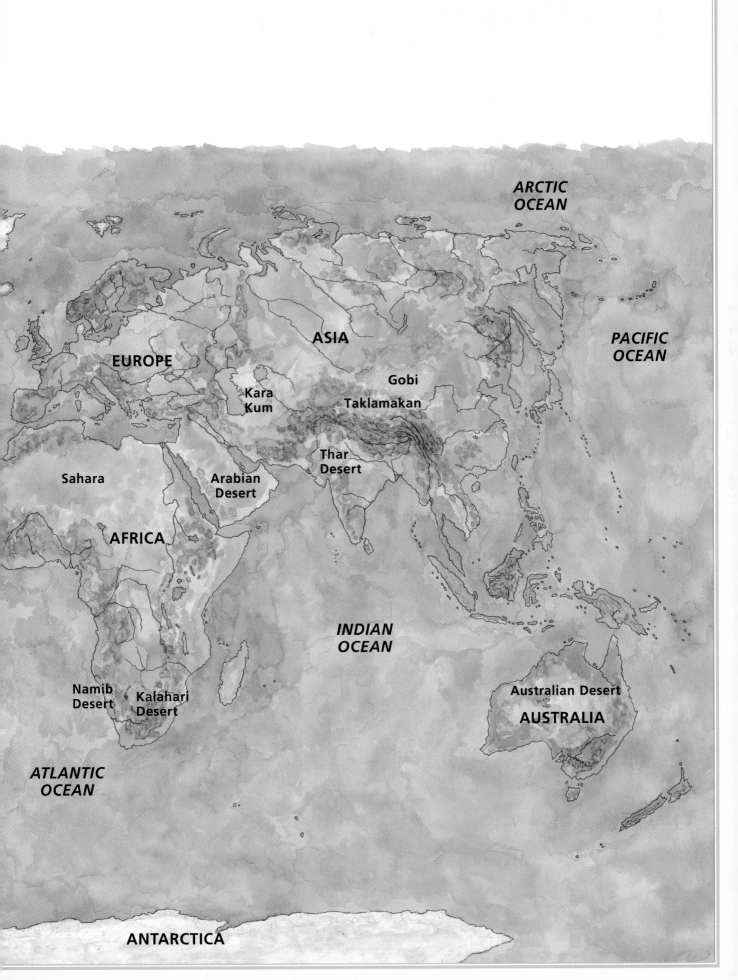

The Sahara

The Sahara is by far the biggest desert in the world. It stretches over 3,100 miles (5,000 km) from the Atlantic Ocean to the Red Sea and covers more than a quarter of the continent of Africa. Its name comes from an Arabic word for desert.

ATLANTIC OCEAN

MEDITERRANEAN SEA

Scorpion

Locust

Nile River

Falcon

Ahaggar Mountains

RED SEA

Oasis

Sandgrouse

Tuareg people

Jerboa

Fennec fox

Arabian camels

Desert hedgehog

Addax

Seas of sand

Some parts of the Sahara are made up of mile after mile of shifting sand dunes. These huge areas of sand are called **ergs**, and in these areas many sand dunes are more than 650 feet (200 m) high. The world's highest sand dunes are in the Algerian part of the Sahara. They are 1,525 feet (465 m) high, which is taller than the Empire State Building in New York.

Winds blow the sand dunes of the Sahara into many different shapes.

Some peaks of the Ahaggar Mountains, in Algeria, are nearly 9,850 feet (3,000 m) high.

Rocks and mountains

Only about a fifth of the Sahara is covered with sand. Some of the desert is made up of flat, stony plains. At its lowest point, the desert is 433 feet (132 m) below sea level. But most of the Sahara is made up of rocky regions called **hammadas**. There are also many high mountains. At the Sahara's highest point in Chad, the Tibesti Mountains rise to 11,205 feet (3,415 m). These mountainous regions have slightly more rain than other parts of the desert, and there is sometimes snow on the peaks.

Living in the desert

The Sahara has about 90 large fertile areas, called oases, where people live in villages and grow crops. There are also many smaller oases that support one or two families each.

Altogether, less than 2 million people live in the Sahara. Many of these are **nomads**, such as the Tuareg of the central uplands. Nomadic people wander the desert, traveling from one oasis to the next.

FACTS

AREA 3,250,000 square miles (8,400,000 sq km)

LOCATION MAP

The Australian Desert

The name *Australian Desert* refers to five desert areas that spread across western and central Australia. They are the Great Sandy, Great Victoria, Simpson, Gibson, and Sturt Stony deserts. These large desert areas are next to one another.

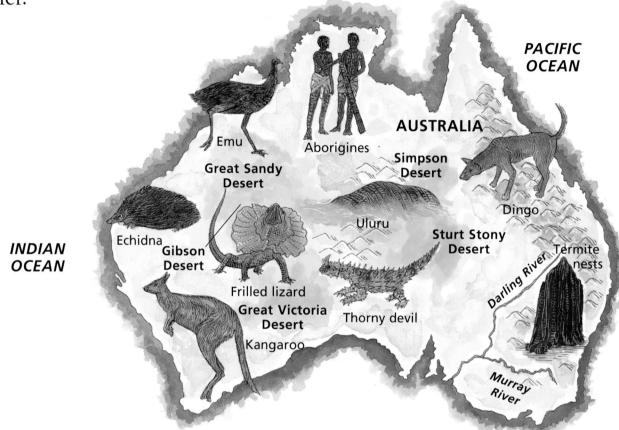

PACIFIC OCEAN

AUSTRALIA

INDIAN OCEAN

Emu

Aborigines

Great Sandy Desert

Simpson Desert

Dingo

Echidna

Uluru

Sturt Stony Desert

Termite nests

Gibson Desert

Darling River

Frilled lizard

Great Victoria Desert

Thorny devil

Kangaroo

Murray River

Desert continent

Deserts cover more than a third of Australia, making it the world's driest continent. But the Australian Desert has a little more rainfall than most other desert regions. This means that many areas have a thin cover of plant life. In years of good rainfall, these areas are used for grazing sheep. In Australia, **bush** areas with small woody plants and some trees are called the **outback**.

This part of the Simpson Desert has a good covering of shrubs and trees.

FACTS

AREA   600,000 square miles
        (1,550,000 sq km)

LOCATION   Central Australia

These Aboriginal children have put on body paint for a dance festival. Many Aborigine customs and ceremonies are thousands of years old.

The first Australians

The Aborigines came to Australia from Asia about 40,000 years ago. They probably crossed land that is now underwater and wandered the desert, hunting and gathering food. Their way of life was in danger when settlers arrived from Europe in the eighteenth century. Now some areas of desert have been set aside as Aboriginal **reserves**.

Runners and jumpers

Many animals in the Australian Desert live nowhere else in the world. Early European explorers were so surprised by **emus** and kangaroos that they described Australia as the land where birds run instead of flying and animals hop instead of running. The emu is a large bird, but it has small wings and cannot fly. It is as tall as a human and can move faster than an Olympic runner. The red kangaroo is even taller and hops along on its huge back legs. It can jump more than 30 feet (9 m) in one leap.

The Arabian Desert

The Arabian Desert covers nearly all of the Arabian Peninsula. This **peninsula**, in southwest Asia, is separated from Africa and the Sahara by the Red Sea. The desert covers parts of five countries and is made up of three different desert areas, called Rub al-Khali, An Nafud, and the Syrian Desert.

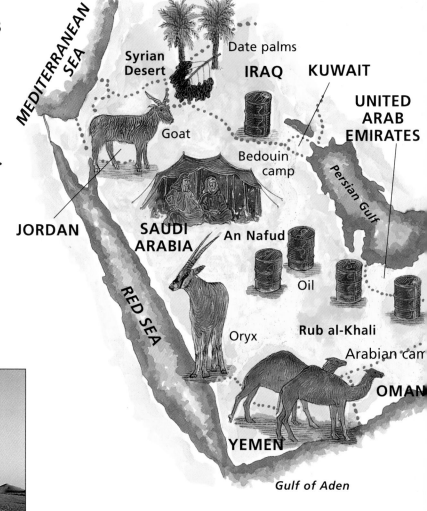

This part of the empty quarter, in northern Yemen, shows clearly how this desert region got its name.

The empty quarter

The desert region called Rub al-Khali, in southern Saudi Arabia, is one of the largest stretches of sand in the world. Its name means "empty quarter." It is so hot and dry that very few people ever go into this wilderness, though some **bedouin** nomads wander along its edges.

A desert's sand forms over millions of years. As rocks are heated rapidly during the day, they **expand**. As they cool rapidly at night, they **contract**. Gradually they begin to crumble and form sand, which is then blown around the desert by the wind. In the Arabian Desert, strong winds from the north carry and move huge loads of sand and dust, constantly changing the landscape.

Ship of the desert

The camel with one hump that lives in the Arabian Peninsula is called a **dromedary**. This large, strong animal is well-suited to life in the desert. Camels store fat in their humps and can go for days without food or water. The fat provides them with **energy**. As they use the fat, their humps get smaller. The dromedary is the main form of transportation across a sea of sand. Because of this, it is often called "the ship of the desert."

FACTS

AREA   500,000 square miles (1,300,000 sq km)

LOCATION   Southwest Asia: parts of Jordan, Oman, Saudi Arabia, United Arab Emirates, and Yemen

An oil refinery in the Arabian Desert. Most of the oil fields are near the Persian Gulf coast. Oil and natural gas are the region's main resources.

Oil beneath the sands

Oil is a very important **resource**. It is sometimes trapped in the rock beneath a desert. The discovery of oil in the Arabian Desert brought a lot of money and many changes to the countries in the region. The largest of these, Saudi Arabia, is the third biggest producer of **crude oil** in the world.

After the oil has been brought to the surface, it is pumped through pipelines to huge ships, called **tankers**, on the coast of the Persian Gulf. The tankers then carry it to other countries around the world.

The Gobi

The Gobi stretches across the borders of Mongolia and China, in Central Asia. Its name comes from a Mongolian word meaning "waterless place." This desert is the farthest north and generally the coldest of the ten biggest deserts. It lies on a **plateau** 2,950 to 4,920 feet (900 to 1,500 m) high.

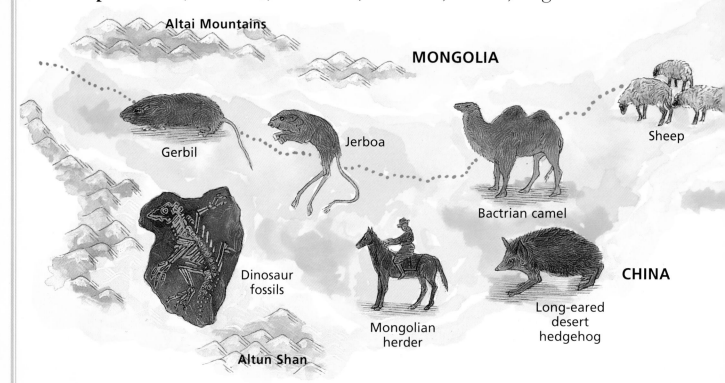

Altai Mountains

MONGOLIA

Gerbil

Jerboa

Sheep

Bactrian camel

Dinosaur fossils

Mongolian herder

Long-eared desert hedgehog

CHINA

Altun Shan

Extreme cold and heat

The Gobi has **extreme** weather. In the winter the temperature drops to -40°F (-40°C). Spring and autumn are dry and cold. But in the summer there are long heat waves, and the temperature can rise to 113°F (45°C) in July. The desert's small amount of rain falls mainly in the warmer months and **evaporates** quickly. This extreme climate has created a rocky wasteland surrounded by dry **grasslands** called **steppes**. There are some high sand dunes in the Gobi, too.

A Mongolian boy herds his cattle across grassland at the edge of the desert.

Land of the dinosaurs

Scientists think that the Gobi may once have had a less extreme climate. We now know that dinosaurs roamed this area millions of years ago. In the 1920s an American scientist went into the desert in search of eagles' nests. He found the nests and also came across some **fossilized** dinosaur eggs that were 95 million years old. This was the first proof that dinosaurs laid eggs. Since then, there have been many successful fossil-hunting expeditions in the Gobi. Parts of a giant dinosaur, called **deinocheirus**, were found there.

Many very old bones have been found in the Mongolian Valley of the Dinosaurs. It is hard work searching and digging in this dry region, and fossil-hunters have to take water with them.

Camels and horses

The Bactrian camel of the Gobi has two humps on its back. It has a long, woolly coat to keep it warm in the winter. In the summer most of this hair falls out. Some Bactrian camels are wild, but most are kept by nomads and herders as working animals.

The Mongols of northern China and Mongolia are expert horse riders. They follow their herds of sheep, goats, and cattle across the desert and surrounding steppes.

FACTS

AREA   400,000 square miles
       (1,040,000 sq km)

LOCATION   Central Asia: southern
       Mongolia and northern China

15

The Kalahari Desert

The Kalahari Desert is a large, dry plain in southern Africa. It covers most of Botswana and spreads into parts of neighboring Namibia and South Africa. Some parts of the Kalahari Desert have more than the usual amount of rain for a desert, especially in the summer. Because of this, there are large areas of grassland and **scrub** within the region.

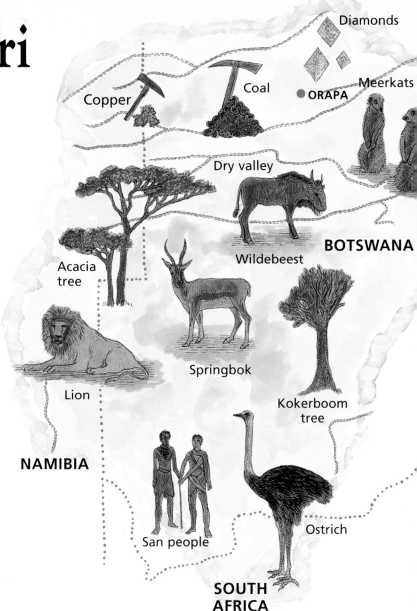

Diamonds

Copper

Coal

ORAPA

Meerkats

Dry valley

Acacia tree

Wildebeest

BOTSWANA

Springbok

Lion

Kokerboom tree

San people

NAMIBIA

Ostrich

SOUTH AFRICA

Dry valleys

In the northern part of the Kalahari Desert, old river valleys can still be seen. In the south, four more dry valleys — the Auob, Kuruman, Molopo, and Nossob — wind their way toward the flowing Orange River. These sandy **riverbeds** are like ghosts. Water only flows down them in the **rainy season** during very wet years.

Some trees manage to survive in the grassland regions of the Kalahari Desert, where there is sometimes rain.

Life in the bush

The San people, or Bushmen, of the Kalahari are nomadic **hunter-gatherers**. They once wandered across most of southern Africa, but today there are probably fewer than 2,000 San living in the desert. The San know how to live in the desert. The men are skillful hunters, using arrows tipped with poison made from beetles. San women and children spend much of their time gathering plants. San children quickly learn the appearance and names of about 200 different plants.

A young San boy tends his fire. The San make shelters from branches covered with dry grasses.

FACTS

AREA   200,000 square miles (520,000 sq km)

LOCATION   Southern Africa: parts of Botswana, Namibia, and South Africa

Desert wildlife

In the Kalahari Gemsbok National Park, **acacia** trees grow in the dry riverbeds. Grass and shrubs provide food for herds of antelopes and **wildebeests**. There are also lions, wild dogs, **jackals**, **meerkats**, **ostriches**, and many other birds. This is a protected area for wildlife. In other parts of the Kalahari Desert, companies have found coal, copper, and other minerals. One of the largest diamond mines in the world is at Orapa, in northern Botswana.

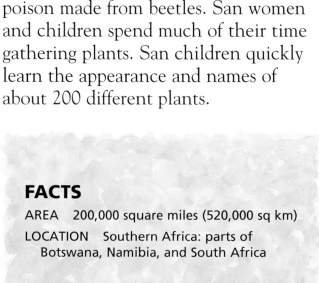

The Taklamakan

The sixth biggest desert in the world, the Taklamakan, has a name that means: "Go in, and you won't come out again." The Taklamakan is in the Xinjiang province of northwest China.

- Jerboa
- Tien Shan
- Silk Road
- Turfan Depression
- Grapes
- CHINA
- KASHI
- Bactrian camels
- Asian wild ass
- Sandgrouse
- Peaches
- Pamir Mountains
- Wheat
- Desert travelers
- Kunlun Shan

The snowcapped Pamir Mountains form a backdrop to the stony wastes of the desert.

High mountains

The Taklamakan reaches a height of 4,920 feet (1,500 m) and is surrounded on three sides by mountain ranges. In the north, the snowcapped Tien Shan, or Heavenly Mountains, separate China from Kyrgyzstan. To the south, the Kunlun Shan divides the desert from Xizang province, while in the west there are the high Pamir Mountains.

In the east, 505 feet (154 m) below sea level, lies a great bowl of dry rock. This is the Turfan Depression, the second lowest area of land on the surface of the Earth.

The old Silk Road

The famous Italian explorer Marco Polo traveled over the Pamir Mountains and around the southern edges of the Taklamakan, at the end of the thirteenth century. He journeyed with his father and his uncle in a **caravan** of camels, horses, and donkeys. They followed the Silk Road. This was the old trade route used by merchants to take precious silk from China to Europe.

In the desert the Polos put up a sign at night, pointing in the direction they were traveling. In the morning, although the landscape looked the same all around them, they knew which way to go.

Mud-brick ruins near the Turfan Depression are all that remain of the town of Gaochang. This was once an important stop for camel caravans on the old Silk Road.

Oasis city

Kashi, at the western end of the desert and at the foot of the Pamir Mountains, grew up around an oasis. It was an important stop for caravans on the old Silk Road and has been fought over by many different peoples. The Chinese first occupied Kashi in the second century B.C., and in 1219 it was won by the Mongols. There are still silk markets in the city.

Kashi is very fertile. It is supplied with water by a river and some wells. Wheat, corn, and rice are grown there, as well as melons, grapes, and peaches.

FACTS

AREA   125,000 square miles
          (320,000 sq km)

LOCATION   Northwest China:
          Xinjiang province

The Sonoran Desert

North America's biggest desert is the seventh largest desert in the world. The Sonoran Desert runs across the border between the United States and Mexico. It covers parts of two states, Arizona and California, as well as three Mexican states, including Sonora.

The modern city of Phoenix, Arizona, stands on old Native American desert lands. Here the ancestors of the Papago and Pima built canals to help them farm the land.

The modern desert

The Sonoran Desert has many different kinds of landscapes. There are large areas of sand dunes, cactus forests, rocky wastes, Native American reservations, and national parks.

A highway runs across the northern part of the desert. It goes from the city of Tucson to Phoenix, the state capital of Arizona. There are about 430,000 people living in Tucson, and Phoenix has more than 2 million people. There are many other smaller towns within the desert region. Those who live there are the modern people of the desert.

Native American desert people

Native Americans have lived in this area for 20,000 years. Five of these groups lived as herders and farmers in the Sonoran Desert. They are the Maricopa, Mohave, Papago, Pima, and Yuma.

Today, 6,000 Native Americans live on the Papago reservation. They lead a modern life but have not forgotten their roots. They call themselves Tohono O'odham, or "desert people." When they lived by gathering food from the desert, their most important yearly festival was a rainmaking **ceremony**. Other groups have their own ceremonies, such as the deer dance of the Yaqui.

Tall saguaro cacti grow among other cacti, grasses, and shrubs in many parts of the Sonoran Desert.

Giant cactus

The Sonoran Desert has 300 different types of cacti, including the saguaro cactus, which is the largest cactus in the world. This giant can grow over 55 feet (17 m) tall — about the height of nine people. Some desert birds find the cactus useful. Gila woodpeckers peck their way into saguaro cacti to make their nest. And when they leave, the tiny elf owl takes its turn in the ready-made hole.

The roadrunner, on the other hand, spends its time on the ground. This bird, a relative of the cuckoo, runs away from danger and will chase anything that moves. It can run at speeds of up to 15 miles per hour (24 kph).

The Namib Desert

The Namib Desert runs in a long strip along the Atlantic coast of Namibia, in southern Africa. It is just a few hundred miles west of the Kalahari Desert. The Namib Desert is one of the world's oldest deserts, dating back 55 million years or more.

Antelope

Skeleton Coast

NAMIBIA

Viper

Shipwreck

ATLANTIC OCEAN

Sand lizard

Darkling beetle

Welwitschia

Orange River

Skeleton Coast

The northern coastline of the Namib Desert is called the Skeleton Coast. Its name comes from the huge number of shipwrecks that have happened there. Thick fog, dangerous ocean currents, howling winds, hidden **reefs**, and rocks have caused these disasters. Stories are told of sailors scrambling ashore, only to die in the dry, hot desert.

A shipwreck shows why this is called the Skeleton Coast. The desert sands are constantly moving and soon bury anything that is washed up by the ocean.

The Namib Desert's inland sand dunes are formed by sand carried from the coast by fierce winds. Trees have sent deep roots down to find water even here. This may be the beginning of a small oasis.

Blooming desert

The strange welwitschia plant, which grows only on gravel plains in the Namib, can live for more than a thousand years. It has a huge 10-foot- (3-m-) long root and two long leaves that look like straps. It takes in water through millions of pores and stores the water in its root. Other desert plants have a very short life. When it rains, they suddenly shoot up. They flower within a few weeks and scatter their seeds before they die.

Sea fog

The Namib Desert has very little rain, but on many days fog rolls in from the ocean. The fog is caused by cold-water currents in the ocean, cooling the warm air above. This gives the desert some water, which helps a number of small animals to survive. Beetles, **termites**, and spiders depend on the fog for water. The fog collects on their bodies and turns to water. Lizards find their water by eating the insects. The insects are then eaten by the viper. The **sidewinding** viper hunts by burying itself in the sand and waiting to strike by putting poison into its **prey** with its fangs.

FACTS

AREA   116,000 square miles (300,000 sq km)

LOCATION   Southwest Africa along the Atlantic coast of Namibia

23

The Kara Kum

The Kara Kum, or "black desert," is in the western part of Central Asia. It lies in Turkmenistan, a country on the Caspian Sea that was part of the Soviet Union until 1991.

ARAL SEA

Oil

Gas

TURKMENISTAN

Carpet

Lizard

Bactrian camel

CASPIAN SEA

Amu Darya River

Cotton

Goat

Wild ass

Sheep

Ashkhabad

Karakumsky Canal

IRAN

Kopetdag mountain range

Desert country

The Kara Kum covers more than half of the country of Turkmenistan. At the southwest corner of the desert, the Kopetdag mountain range forms the border with Iran. These rugged mountains tower over the Turkmenistan capital city, Ashkhabad. Local people call the **foothills** "moon mountains," because they are almost completely bare. Strong earthquakes shake this region and are gradually pushing the mountains higher.

The rocky peaks of the Kopetdag mountain range rise up at the edge of the desert.

24

Industry and agriculture

The Kara Kum is rich in oil and natural gas, and the region's chemical and mining **industries** have grown in recent years. In the oases people grow cotton and raise sheep and horses. The karakul sheep that live in the desert have black, gray, or brown coats. Wool from the lambs is especially valuable.

Irrigation has created oases and helped farmers. The biggest waterway is the Karakumsky Canal. It runs more than 620 miles (1,000 km) from the Amu Darya River to the foothills of the Kopetdag mountain range.

Flocks of karakul sheep are herded by Turkoman people, mainly for their lambs. The curly fur of karakul lambs is often called Persian lamb.

Turkoman people

The Turkoman were once nomadic people. They lived in tents with round tops and wandered the edges of the Kara Kum. A few still live for part of the year in tents, moving when they need to find new land to graze their herds of goats, sheep, and camels. They are Muslims, followers of the religion of Islam.

The Turkoman are famous for making carpets with beautiful designs. Many of the carpets are now woven in factories and are important to the **economy** of Turkmenistan.

FACTS

AREA 105,000 square miles
(270,000 sq km)

LOCATION West Central Asia: Turkmenistan

25

The Thar Desert

The Thar Desert, also called the Great Indian Desert, is a region of rolling sand hills in northwest India and Pakistan. It is the tenth biggest desert in the world and covers most of the Indian state of Rajasthan.

Gazelle

PAKISTAN

Indira Gandhi Canal

Great bustard

Bikaner

Jaisalmer

Camel caravan

Wild ass

ARABIAN SEA

INDIA

Rajasthani people

The desert town of Jaisalmer, viewed from the top of the town's old fort. Hindu warriors built many forts in Rajasthan hundreds of years ago.

Watering the desert

There is little water in the Thar Desert. Almost all the year's rain falls in just three months, from July to September. Rainwater is collected in tanks and **reservoirs**, and many canals have been built to take water across the desert. The biggest is the Indira Gandhi Canal. It carries water 403 miles (649 km) from the north and irrigates the areas around the desert towns of Bikaner and Jaisalmer. When there is water, farmers grow crops such as wheat, cotton, and sugarcane. But there are often severe **droughts**.

Travel by camel

There are railroads and dusty roads across the Thar Desert, but many people living in the desert prefer to travel by camel. Visitors to Jaisalmer can go on a camel expedition into the desert. The 186-mile (300-km) journey to Bikaner takes 11 days. There is usually one camel per person, plus one each for baggage. Desert riders on these trips have to take water bottles, suntan lotion, a large hat, sunglasses, and a soft pillow to sit on. At Jaisalmer, there is also a desert festival every February, with dancing, camel races, and camel polo.

FACTS

AREA   100,000 square miles (260,000 sq km)

LOCATION   Indian subcontinent: across the state of Rajasthan in India and the Sind province in Pakistan

Rajasthani women collect firewood. Irrigation canals have helped plants to grow in the Thar region, but wood is still scarce.

The spreading desert

Over the last 10,000 years, the Thar Desert has been growing. This may be because of changes in the climate of the region, especially the wind direction. But people have also helped to speed up the growth of the desert. For example, in the 1970s many of the forests in India, in the areas around the desert, were cut down. Once trees have gone, the unprotected soil dries quickly and is blown away by the wind.

The World's Deserts

The world's main hot deserts are found in two bands that stretch around the Earth. One band is north of the equator and follows the line of the Tropic of Cancer. This includes the Sahara and the Arabian Desert. The other band lies along the Tropic of Capricorn, and this includes the Australian and the Kalahari deserts. There are many other deserts in the world.

The Atacama Desert

The Atacama Desert (shown right) stretches for almost 620 miles (1,000 km) along the Pacific coast of northern Chile, in South America. It covers an area of 69,500 square miles (180,000 sq km) and is probably the driest region on Earth. Few plants grow here, and the windblown landscape is covered with salt, left behind as water evaporates.

The Mojave Desert

Plants in the Mojave Desert, in southern California, bloom in spring. A beavertail cactus (shown left) shows its beautiful flowers, though these will not last for very long. The Mojave Desert, which covers an area of about 13,515 square miles (35,000 sq km), is almost completely surrounded by mountains. To the north is Death Valley, the hottest and driest place in North America. In some parts of the desert, people driving trucks have caused dust storms over 20 miles (30 km) long. To the south is another dry area, the Colorado Desert. A solar tower, which uses sunlight reflected off mirrors to produce energy, is located in the Mojave Desert.

Antarctica

The continent of Antarctica (shown above), where the South Pole is located, is sometimes called an ice desert. This white wasteland is more than one and a half times the size of the Sahara. A thick ice sheet covers the region, which is the coldest and windiest place on Earth.

The average temperature in parts of the Antarctic is -72°F (-58°C). In the winter, strong winds blow across the ice at up to 200 miles per hour (320 kph). There are several scientific bases in Antarctica. The region is protected by a treaty between many countries.

East Africa

Life is hard for the people of the desert regions of northern Kenya (shown left), Somalia, and Ethiopia. The area has very few plants, and in recent years East African countries have been hit by terrible droughts and **famines**. In Somalia, civil war has made life in the desert even harder.

Glossary

acacia A tree that grows in warm areas

bedouin Arabs who wander the Arabian Desert and parts of the Sahara

bush Land partly covered with low plants and some trees

caravan A group traveling together

ceremony A celebration of an event

contract To become smaller

crude oil Oil in its natural state

deinocheirus A large dinosaur with huge, vicious claws

desertification The process of land becoming desert

dromedary An Arabian camel with one hump

Kangaroos in their desert environment

Tuareg crossing the desert on their camels

drought A period of little or no rain

economy A country's management of its wealth

emu A large bird from Australia

energy The ability to act or do work

environment The place where people, animals, or plants live

erg An area of shifting mounds of sand

evaporate To change from a liquid to a gas

expand To grow bigger

extreme Very great

famine A great lack of food in an area

foothills The lower slopes of a mountain

fossilize To preserve the remains of once-living things

grassland An area of land covered with grass

hammada A rocky region

hunter-gatherers People who live by hunting wild animals and gathering fruit, roots, and berries

industry A business that provides a product or service

irrigation Watering the land

jackal A wild animal of Africa similar to a coyote or dog

landscape An area of land and its special qualities

meerkat A small, gray animal with black markings and a slender body

nomads People who wander from place to place to find food and grazing land for their animals

ostrich A large bird from Africa that cannot fly but can run very fast

outback The part of Australia that is partly covered with low plants and some trees

peninsula A strip of land that sticks out into the ocean

plain Flat land with few trees

plateau A flat area of high land

prey An animal that is hunted by another animal for food

rainy season The time of year when a lot of rain falls

reef A strip of rock, sand, or coral near the surface of the ocean

reserve An area set aside to protect the plants and animals that live there

reservoir A large lake used to collect and store water

resource Something that people can use to live on, or that can bring wealth when sold to others

riverbed The land between the banks of a river that is usually covered with water

sand dune A high mound of sand

scrub An area of scattered bushes, small trees, and other plants in a dry region

Lions resting in the desert scrub

sidewinding Moving forward with a sideways, looping motion

steppe A large grassy area

tanker A ship that has tanks to hold liquids

termite An insect that eats wood

wasteland An empty place where few plants or animals can live

wildebeest An African antelope with a head like an ox

Camels arriving at an oasis in the desert

Index

Words in **bold** appear in the glossary on pages 30–31.